CEO Guide to Doing Business in South Africa

By Ade Asefeso MCIPS MBA

Second Edition

ISBN-13: 978-1499584059

ISBN-10: 1499584059

Publisher: AA Global Sourcing Ltd
Website: http://www.aaglobalsourcing.com

Table of Contents

Disclaimer

This publication is designed to provide competent and reliable information regarding the subject matter covered. However, it is sold with the understanding that the author and publisher are not engaged in rendering professional advice. The authors and publishers specifically disclaim any liability that is incurred from the use or application of contents of this book.

If you purchased this book without a cover you should be aware that this book may have been stolen property and reported as "unsold and destroyed" to the publisher. In this case neither the author nor the publisher has received any payment for this "stripped book."

Dedication

This book is dedicated to the hundreds of thousands of incredible souls in the world who have weathered through the up and down of recent recession.

To my family and friends who seems to have been sent here to teach me something about who I am supposed to be. They have nurtured me, challenged me, and even opposed me.... But at every juncture has taught me!

This book is dedicated to my lovely boys, Thomas, Michael and Karl. Teaching them to manage their finance will give them the lives they deserve. They have taught me more about life, presence, and energy management than anything I have done in my life.

Chapter 1: Introduction

Trade Organization; have helped South Africa become a player in the global trading system. Trade reforms, such as tariff reductions and a rationalisation programme, have been introduced.

Market access has been enhanced through free trade agreements with the European Union and the Southern African Development Community (SADC).

UK has identified South Africa as a high-growth market. The UK is one of South Africa's most significant trading partners, with over £7 billion in two-way trade in goods and services. With a climate that is geared for growth and open for trade, South Africa is the ideal destination for the investor who has an eye on building a global empire.

AA Global Sourcing Ltd http://www.aaglobalsourcing.com is the organisation that helps UK-based companies succeeds in the global economy. We also help overseas companies bring their high quality investment to the UK's dynamic economy; acknowledged as Europe's best place from which to succeed in global business. We provide companies with the tools they require to be competitive on the world stage.

South Africa is a sophisticated and promising market, offering a combination of well-developed First World economic infrastructure with a vibrant emerging market economy.

Since the current government came to power in 1994 the country has made tremendous strides towards becoming a major contributor in international markets.

South Africa has abundant natural resources, a well developed banking system, good infrastructure with major capital injections to upgrade this further, a reasonable tax structure, a business culture that is not too dissimilar from that of the UK, with a time difference of only one or two hours, a fairly stable political climate, a stock exchange ranked among the top 20 in the world, and is the gateway to other African markets.

The country has previously hosted cricket world cup, rugby world cup and 2010 FIFA world cup tournaments.

South Africa was ranked as the eighteenth most attractive destination for foreign direct investment, by global strategic management consulting firm AT Kearney and ranked in the top four countries in terms of the transparency surrounding its budgets, according to the Open Budget Index.

In comparison to other BRIC nations (Brazil, Russia, India, China), South Africa is spending two to three times more on education – 7.18 per cent of its GDP. Unit labour costs in South Africa are significantly lower than those of many other emerging markets.

South Africa signed The Global Agreement on Tariffs and Trade in 1994, and became a member of the World Trade Organisation.

Chapter 2: Why South Africa?

Often, new exporters will feel a bit overwhelmed about trading with South Africa. Much consideration and planning will need to go into deciding on the company type, delivery of products and services, marketing strategies, and local conditions.

Before making these big decisions exporters and investors should spend some time thinking about business objectives:

The questions listed below should help you to focus your thoughts. Your answers to them will highlight areas for further research and also suggest a way forward that is right for your company.

Your Aim:
- Do you wish to sell to South Africa?
- Do you wish to establish your own company presence in South Africa for example through a representative office or limited liability company?
- Do you need to be involved in South Africa at all?

Your Company:
- What are the unique selling points (features and benefits) for your product or service?
- Do you know if there is a market for your product or service in South Africa?
- Do you know if you can be competitive in South Africa?

- Do you have the time and resources to handle the demand of communication, travel, product delivery and after sales service?

Your Knowledge:
- Do you know how to secure payment for your products or service?
- Do you know where in South Africa you should start?
- Do you know how to locate and screen potential partners, agents or distributors?
- Do you know about broad-based black economic empowerment legislation and how it could affect your business?

You may then want to use all of the above questions as a basis for developing a formal strategy, although this will not be necessary or appropriate for all companies. This book will take you through the process of doing business with South Africa

Who is this book for?

This book is aimed at companies experienced in overseas trade who are new to doing business with South Africa. Your company may be an exporter looking to sell directly to South African customers or through an agent or distributor in South Africa. Alternatively, you may be planning to set up a representative office, joint venture or other form of permanent presence in South Africa.

This book aims to provide a route map of the way ahead, together with signposts to sources of help. It identifies the main issues associated with initial research, market entry, risk management and cultural issues. It also includes questions you should ask at the beginning of your research into South Africa.

We do not pretend to provide all the answers in this book, however it will point you in the direction of the people, organisations and publications that will be able to answer these and many other questions.

The objective of this book is to steer companies through the initial research and preparation stages of entering the South African market. It is far better to spend time and money in carrying out thorough research and preparation before entering the market than to enter South Africa in a hurry, not wishing to miss the boat, only to discover that you have made a very costly mistake.

Chapter 3: South Africa Regional Considerations

South Africa is a country of great diversity, not just in terms of the people, but also in terms of trade and investment opportunities.

Whether it's a wine farm in the Western Cape, a finance firm in Gauteng, or manufacturing plant in KwaZulu-Natal, there is high potential for solid returns on investments.

This chapter will briefly cover some regional considerations for those who wish to expand their operations to South Africa. The three provinces of Gauteng, KwaZulu-Natal and the Western Cape account for 65 per cent of the country's gross domestic product (GDP).

Gauteng

The Gauteng province is the economic hub of South Africa. It is the smallest in terms of size – 1.4 per cent of land area; yet it contributes about 34 per cent of its GDP. Johannesburg is the most important city in the province in terms of investment, though Tshwane (formerly Pretoria), Ekurhuleni and the Vaal Triangle all have sound sector-specific options.

Johannesburg is just over 120 years old. Estimates are that by 2015 Johannesburg's borders will have grown to the extent that they reach neighbouring Tshwane and Ekurhuleni. This polycentric urban region will have approximately 14.6 million people, making it one of the largest cities in the world.

Though the city was founded on gold mining, in recent decades businesses have diversified. The finance, IT, real estate, media, private healthcare, and transport sectors coupled with a booming leisure activities market provide a cornucopia of profitable ventures for start-up businesses.

The manufacturing and construction industries are experiencing a boom. Large-scale urbanisation coupled with the 2010 FIFA World Cup have ensured that steel manufacturers, cement producers and infrastructure development companies have all been doing well.

For information on how the Gauteng Economic Development Agency (GEDA) can help visit www.geda.co.za

Western Cape

The Western Cape is a diverse province that can offer investors opportunities in multiple sectors. The province is important in terms of the South African economy, as it provides almost 15 per cent to South Africa's GDP.

It is a wealthy, rapidly growing province that prides itself on being a leader in terms of technology. The ICT sector is experiencing a boom, as many businesses locate in the Western Cape to take advantage of the skill base that exists in the province.

The Western Cape is steadily consolidating its position as a hot bed for creative industries and design. Fashion items, jewellery and crafts produced in the province are of high quality and are exported to European and American markets.

In a decade, the film industry has grown from five production companies and 50 crew members to about 150 companies and 1,650 crew. A number of major international productions have used the areas within the Western Cape as a film location.

The primary city in terms of business activity is Cape Town. Insurance companies, retail groups, publishers, design houses, fashion designers, shipping companies, petrochemical companies, architects and advertising agencies are among the commercial industries that the city is host to.

For further information from the Investment and Trade Promotion Agency for the Western Cape (Wesgro) visit
www.wesgro.co.za

KwaZulu-Natal

The KwaZulu-Natal (KZN) province, which contributes almost 17 per cent to South Africa's GDP, is home to Durban and Richards Bay, two of the largest ports on the African continent. Most of the economic activity is based around these two ports and Pietermaritzburg, the capital city of the province.

Durban is the third most populous city in South Africa and can stake claim to being the busiest container port in Africa. It is a suitable investment destination as it has a large human resource base, a high growth rate and already houses a stable business base.

Richards Bay has large scale industrialisation. This is due to the harbour and availability of natural resources. The port is the largest deep-water port in Africa, and handles over 75 million tonnes of cargo each year.

Pietermaritzburg and the surrounds contribute 11 per cent of the provincial GDP. The municipality offers a number of incentives to investors, such as discounts on electricity, rebates on rates and discounted refuse removal rates.

Pietermaritzburg's proximity to the port of Durban, the airport, and main route between KZN and Johannesburg give it a logistical advantage.

KZN's manufacturing sector is the second largest in the country. It also offers opportunities in transport, communications, printing and publishing, food and beverage production, nonelectrical machinery, iron and steel, textiles and finance. The agricultural sector is also an important one in the province, with 6.5 million hectares of land being used for farming purposes.

KZN province is one in which growth is being experienced across multiple sectors. The petroleum and chemical products industry has grown by 50 per cent in the last decade. The transport equipment industry has experienced growth of 52 per cent in the same period.

For further information on Trade & Investment KwaZulu-Natal (TIKZN) visit www.tikzn.co.za

AA Global Sourcing Ltd http://www.aaglobalsourcing.com provides a wide variety of private sector advice for companies wishing to do business in South Africa.

This ranges from the business services provided by the big international professional services firms to specific services provided by specialist operators.

The range of services available from AA Global Sourcing Ltd includes company structuring advice, marketing, website design, partner selection, due diligence, legal services, advice on intellectual property rights and outsourcing. They also offer more in-depth assistance on developing a strategy for South Africa and operational management.

The importance of good quality independent legal advice, as in any foreign market, cannot be emphasised enough. It is essential to take this into consideration at the early stages of doing business in South Africa. Always seek good-quality independent legal advice before starting or signing anything that could have legal implications for your company, such as contracts or representation agreements.

Specialist legal advice on intellectual property rights protection is also recommended and there are a number of highly qualified patent agent firms available. Legal advice can be expensive, but it is money well spent. It is far better to ensure that your interests in South Africa are fully protected than to leave yourself vulnerable to untoward consequences; which can be even more expensive to sort out.

Chapter 4: Finding the Right Agent or Distributor

Two of the most common market entry methods into overseas markets are via agents or distributors. They know the market in their territory and can potentially offer a quick way to building market share. The two are often confused, but the differences are very straightforward.

Agents:

Work for a commission, never buy or own the products, and can be controlled by you.

Distributors:

Buy and sell to make a profit, own the products, and cannot be controlled by you.

One of the frequent queries is, "Which should I choose, agent or distributor?"

There are no hard-and-fast rules, and the answer may well be different for different territories.

The checklist below details things you should bear in mind when looking for a suitable agent or distributor.

Background:
- Size of agency
- History of agency

- Number of salespeople, their length of service and qualifications
- Other agencies held and success record
- Banking and trade references

Distribution
- Geographical coverage
- Types of outlets covered and frequency of calling
- Transportation
- Warehousing

Are they right for your product?
- Knowledge of local market conditions
- Marketing competence
- Agent's interest in and enthusiasm for new products and yours in particular
- After-sales service levels
- Required skills of salespeople

Once you have chosen an agent or distributor, you will want to ensure that your products receive at least a fair share of the agent's attention.

This can be achieved by:
- Visiting as regularly as is practicable at senior management level – this shows interest in, and commitment to, the agent and the market. This will also provide you with an opportunity to learn about conditions in the market and see how your products are faring.

- Working closely with the agents to show them how they can profit from your products.
- Helping to prepare marketing and sales plans for the agent.
- Linking performance to incentives and agreeing milestone targets.

Chapter 5: Establishing a Permanent Presence

If you are looking to take your business operations to South Africa, you will be pleased to find out that the country has a solid, well regulated company law regime. Various Acts have been put into place that regulates formation, conducting of affairs and liquidation of companies. The companies Act of 1973 does not distinguish between locally owned or foreign based companies.

Close corporations

Close corporations are a popular company type, as the process of setting one up is uncomplicated and comparatively inexpensive. The close corporation will have a separate legal personality and a measure of limited liability.

Partnerships

Partnerships are suitable for taxation purposes, and are often used when organisations are planning to create a joint venture.

Investors should make sure that they fully understand any contractual agreement they enter into with a partner. The roles and responsibilities need to be clearly set out before the business begins operation.

Joint ventures

Joint ventures form the basis of most international operations in South Africa. Larger corporations tend to favour this type of setup.

Franchising

Franchises are an increasingly popular choice for international investors. The franchise industry employs over 250,000 people. Foreign investors tend to enter into a franchise agreement with a South African entity which will then conclude franchise agreements with a number of local franchisees.

There are few laws that dictate how franchise operations should run. However, this may lead to abuse of agreements. Self-regulation seems to be the way in which this is overcome.

The South African Franchise Association has a code of ethics, but there is no obligation to belong to this organisation.

Acquiring an existing company in South Africa

You may also wish to consider partially or wholly acquiring an existing company in South Africa, as there is no legal impediment to this course of action.

Business types

Choice is the keyword when it comes to setting up a business in South Africa. There are several types of companies that can be established. Various factors will influence the company type one sets up. A brief description of company types is given below.

Limited liability companies

A limited liability company allows great flexibility and is often the preferred choice for joint ventures. Limited liability companies have two types: private and public.
The aforementioned Companies Act of 1973 is used in setting up and governing these types of companies.
For further information visit www.cipro.co.za

Branches

As an investor, you may take the decision not to incorporate a subsidiary in South Africa. The best option then is to set up a branch office.

In addition, the approaches below are suitable for companies whose objective is exporting:

- Advertise in professional newspapers, magazines and journals. This can be beneficial for high-tech companies with leading-edge solutions, but less effective for companies without a technical background.
- Consider holding a technical seminar or product introduction meeting to attract potential customers in South Africa. As part of our chargeable services, AA Global Sourcing Ltd can help you organise product promotion events and

identify the audience you need to target.
http://www.aaglobalsourcing.com

- Attend trade shows and exhibitions. Numerous trade shows and exhibitions take place in South Africa throughout the year and these can be an excellent way to meet potential customers face to face.

Chapter 6: Finding a Customer or Partner

Once you have identified where you would like to start and the best market entry option for your company, the next step is to find potential customer or partners.

South African business and legal systems are similar to those found in the UK. Labour law is governed by a number of Acts that provide a framework for businesses to operate in.

Below is a brief list of some labour Acts you will need to be familiar with before trading in South Africa.

1. Basic Conditions of Employment: This Act is to be understood by both employers and employees. It regulates leave, working hours, employment contracts, deductions, pay slips, and termination.

2. Compensation for Occupational Injuries and Diseases:
Injured or ill workers may be eligible for compensation. Understanding the conditions of this Act will ensure that employers know where their responsibilities start and end.

3. Labour Relations: The Labour Relations Act applies to workers and employers. The Act aims to advance economic development and social justice while promoting labour peace and democracy in the workplace.

4. Occupational Health and Safety: Occupational health and safety Acts such as this are common throughout the world. Ignoring the guidelines set out in these Acts is ill-advised.

5. Skills Development: Skills development is an important issue in South Africa. Anyone who wishes to start a business and employ people needs to be aware of the responsibilities they have towards improving the skills of the workforce.

To gain a better understanding of the Acts and how they will impact on trade and investment, visit the Department of Labour website www.labour.gov.za

Investment Promotion and Protection Agreement

Investment Promotion and Protection Agreements (IPPA) are designed to encourage investor confidence by setting high standards of investor protection applicable in international law. Key elements include provisions for equal and non discriminatory treatment of investors and their investments, compensation for expropriation, transfer of capital and returns, and access to independent settlement of disputes. The UK and South Africa signed and ratified an IPPA in 1998.

Marketing

Trade shows, exhibitions and advertising have been identified as ways of meeting potential customers, but you still need to persuade them to buy your product. You will need to ensure that your sales literature is effective in English and whether advertising is appropriate.

We recommend that you consider using a marketing specialist to market your products and advise if you need to adapt your product to meet South African preferences or requirements in order to be able to sell it. Ignoring local regulations, tastes and cultural preferences is a recipe for failure.

Consider your unique selling proposition aspects of your product that differentiate it from similar products in the market.

The South African advertising industry serves a diverse and dynamic market thriving in all sectors, from print and broadcast to outdoor and electronic advertising. A wide range and sophisticated choice of media options are available to marketing and media specialists in line with the latest international media trends.

International advertising agencies are well represented, usually through affiliated networks and local partners. Locally based agencies also have a strong market presence. There are over 400 trade and technical publications in South Africa.

These are specialised journals covering over 50 industrial/speciality categories. These publications offer an excellent opportunity to reach a targeted industrial audience.

For further information visit the Advertising Standards Authority of South Africa website, www.asasa.org.za

Chapter 7: Due Diligence, Branding and Communications

Due Diligence

Due diligence is a security measure that companies often choose to undertake in order to check the viability of potential new businesses or partners, before contracts are signed.

It is vital that companies consider carrying out a fully comprehensive due diligence check on a South African company they plan to do business with such as acquisitions of a shareholding interest, building up an accurate picture of the company is important to safeguard your investment. If you are trying to acquire a local company then it would be advisable to seek the assistance of a professional firm with a presence in South Africa.

There are different levels of due diligence that are appropriate for different situations. If your sole interest is in exporting, the best proof of a South African company's ability to pay is whether it is able to raise a letter of credit from the bank. If so, you do not need to check the company's financial standing as the bank will have already done so, although the reliability of this may depend on who their bankers are.

If you want to establish a business relationship that goes beyond exporting, you will need to carry out further research. A thorough evaluation of your potential partner may be time-consuming and expensive, but doing so will greatly reduce the risk of serious problems in the future. At the macro level due diligence is broken into the broad headings comprising; legal, financial and technical aspects. The technical aspects are best done by you.

As labour laws in South Africa have a lot of bite, companies are also advised to ensure that particular attention is paid to HR issues. For practical purposes, it is recommended that due diligence covers all accounting, tax and legal issues concerning a particular business enterprise.

Branding

Your brand is the central point that connects your customers to your business. It clarifies thinking, defines behaviour, increases business efficiency and will give you a competitive advantage.

Great brands are built by a differentiated strategy, a strong reputation, excellent brand communication and an experience that lives up to the brand promise.

It is therefore advisable to spend some time on getting this right. The name is, after all, the first thing your potential customer will see. Registering your brand or trademark in the UK does not protect it in South Africa.

Day-to-day communications

English is the language of commerce, banking, government and official documentation. It is the dominant business language and is spoken throughout the country.

South African business people expect regular contact from their business clients. You should devote a proportion of your time to developing and maintaining a good relationship with your South African partner. It is important to understand your partner, and time taken getting to know them is time well spent.

Faxes are still popular in South Africa. Modern telecommunications and IT work well in South Africa and it would prove cost-effective to visit the market.

Chapter 8: Certification, Standards and Intellectual Property

Certification and Standards

South Africa is a member of the World Trade Organization (WTO) and follows the Harmonized System (HS) of import classification. Free trade between South Africa and the European Union is increasing as a result of a Free Trade Agreement.

The South Africa Department of Trade and Industry is also empowered to regulate, prohibit or ration imports to South Africa in the national interest, but most goods may be imported into the country without restrictions.

Import permits are required only for specific categories of goods and are obtainable from the Director of Imports and Exports Control. Importers must possess an import permit prior to the date of shipment. Failure to produce a required permit could result in the imposition of penalties.

Some imports may require permission from the Department of Agriculture, Health or Environmental Affairs. Standards are administered by the South African Bureau of Standards (SABS). SABS develops and administers a number of national standards for the purpose of consumer protection, health, safety and environmental issues.

The scope of its work includes chemical and biological standards, electro-technical standards, fibre technology standards, mechanical, transportation and civil engineering standards, and systems standards.

Intellectual Property Rights

IP rights are territorial, that is they only give protection in the countries where they are granted or registered. If you are thinking about trading internationally, then you should consider registering your IP rights in your export markets.

In 2008, South Africa enacted the IPR Intellectual Property Right for Publicly Financed Research and Development Act. The law clarifies obligations related to the ownership of intellectual property rights in the country and applies to aesthetic and functional designs, marks related to patentable inventions and copyright. Further information can be viewed at the South African Department of Trade & Industry's website.

Entering a foreign market poses some challenges in ensuring that your intellectual property rights (IPR) are protected. As we mentioned earlier in this chapter IPR are territorial, hence they only give protection in the countries where they are granted or registered. If you are thinking about trading internationally then you should consider registering your IPR in each country in which you want protection.

An independent intellectual property rights lawyer is invaluable in helping you to establish the best strategy for your company.

The UK Intellectual Property Office (www.ipo.gov.uk) and the British Library Business & IP Centre (www.bl.uk) have further guidance.

IPR theft and protection is not a major issue in South Africa. However, there is small-scale pirating of DVDs, etc. The South African Government and the police are trying to keep this problem under control. South Africa offers well regulated and accessible IPR protection and its International IPR laws are equally well enforced.

South Africa is a member of the Paris Union and acceded to the Stockholm text of the Paris Convention for the protection of intellectual property. South Africa is also a member of the World Intellectual Property Organization (WIPO). The South African Government passed two IPR-related bills in parliament at the end of 1997 – the Counterfeit Goods Act and the Intellectual Property Laws Amendment Bill, thereby enhancing its IPR protection. For further information visit www.cipro.co.za

Chapter 9: Documentation and Getting Paid

Documentation

The Applied Tariff Database section allows users to enter an HS code or product description to obtain tariff rate and details of taxes applicable, enabling you to calculate a landed cost.

The Exporter's Guide to Import Formalities database (searchable by HS code or by product), gives an overview of import procedures and documents, as well as any general and specific requirements for a product. The customary minimum content for each document is also shown.

The Sanitary and Phytosanitary Database facilitates the identification of sanitary and phytosanitary export problems with any non-EU country.

Export controls

Export controls apply to goods upon which the UK Government has placed export licensing requirements. Typically, export controls relate to goods that may be used in some way for military applications, goods of national heritage (e.g. works of art), and certain chemicals used in the production of controlled drugs.

The Export Control Organisation helpline, at the Department for Business, Enterprise & Regulatory Reform, is the first point of contact for information on export controls. The helpline provides advice on many issues, including how to establish whether or not specific goods need an export licence, the different types of export licences, how to complete export licence application forms and how long they take to process. For further information call +44 (0)20 7215 4594 or visit www.berr.gov.uk

A complete and accurate set of documents, completed in English, are vital to avoid delays in processing your goods. The metric system must be used in documentation for South Africa. All goods should be correctly classified, using the Harmonized System (HS) of Tariff Classification.

In general, the following documentation is required for exports to South Africa:
- Customs Import Declaration
- Commercial Invoice
- Packing List
- Certificate of Origin
- Movement Certificate (EUR.1)
- Air Waybill
- Bill of Lading
- Registration on the Manifest Acquittal System (Air Cargo)
- Registration on the Manifest Acquittal System (Sea Cargo)
- Registration with the South African Revenue Service

- Inward/Outward Report for Aircraft
- Inward/Outward Report for Ships
- Supplier's Declaration Sanitary certificates are mandatory for various specified plant and animal products.

The European Commission's Market Access Database is a free tool designed to assist exporters and can only be accessed through an internet service provider based in the EU:

- It provides information on trade barriers which may affect you in overseas markets.

Further information on documentation requirements, export procedures and tariffs can be found on the following websites:
Market Access Database: http://mkaccdb.eu.int/
HM Revenue & Customs: www.hmrc.gov.uk
SITPRO: www.sitpro.org.uk

Getting Paid

Open Account and Bills for Collection are other payment methods commonly used between UK exporters and South African importers, when a trustworthy relationship between the two parties has been developed. Major exports and those requiring long-term finance will require specialist payment and financing.

Regulations regarding exchange control and remittance of currency have to be strictly adhered to by the South African importer, so the UK exporter will have to ensure that correct documentation is supplied to their customer.

Exchange controls are administered by the South African Reserve Bank's Exchange Control Department and through commercial banks authorised to deal in foreign exchange.

All international commercial transactions must be accounted for through these authorised foreign exchange dealers. When exporting to South Africa normal commercial rules should be followed.

At an early stage during negotiations with your importer, discuss with your bank the terms and arrangements for security of payment. You could approach the international department of your UK bank, the UK offices of South African banks or UK-based banks that have offices in South Africa.

If you are a first-time exporter to South Africa, the standard method of receiving payment for your goods is by confirmed documentary letter of credit. The opening of the documentary letter of credit is based on the contract signed between the South African buyer and the foreign seller.

There are no problems regarding letters of credit opened by South African banks being accepted by foreign banks. The South African bank will make payment, provided that the requirements of the letter of credit are met. However, be aware that a letter of credit is a form of contract between two banks.

A bank will make payment provided that the documents submitted to it are in strict compliance with the conditions of the letter of credit. This is regardless of the purchase contract.

To prevent the possibility of a payment being made if the terms of the purchase contract are not met, the seller should check the letter of credit against the terms of the purchase contract and request amendments from the buyer.

If you are a first time exporter to South Africa, the standard method of receiving payment for your goods is by confirmed documentary letter of credit.

Chapter 10: Pricing and Insurance

Pricing

Investors in South Africa will find that the cost of manufacture is low due to the availability of inexpensive labour, rent and accommodation.

Inco terms are international rules that are accepted by governments, legal authorities and practitioners worldwide for the interpretation of the most commonly used terms in international trade.

The International Chamber of Commerce website has information on Inco terms 2000 and defines 13 Inco terms used in foreign trade, for example FOB, CIF, etc. International quotations will normally be based on these terms.

The Institute of Export (www.export.org.uk) offers training on this and other aspects of exporting. South African companies accept pricing in sterling or rands. In recent years the rand has been unstable and hence your customer may be interested in exploring other currency options. In essence, quoting for business in overseas markets is no different from quoting for business in the domestic market.

Typically, the costs to include in your quotation are as follows:
- Costs of raw materials – include all components, labelling and packing costs.

- Manufacturing costs – include all production costs, particularly labour costs.
- Overheads – running costs, depreciation, rent, utilities and transport costs.
- Profit margin – this may vary depending on whether you are trading in a buyer's or seller's market. Profit margins may also be affected by the flexibility of demand for your product (the more flexible the demand, the greater the possibility of increasing sales – but at the right price).

In essence, quoting for business in overseas market is no different from quoting for business in the domestic market.

Insurance

The private sector provides insurance for exports of consumer goods, raw materials and other similar goods. Speak to your banker or insurance broker for more information, or contact the British Insurance Brokers' Association (BIBA) for impartial advice on +44 (0)870 950 1790 or visit www.biba.org.uk

However, private sector insurance has some limitations, particularly for sales of capital goods, major services and construction projects that require longer credit packages or are in riskier markets. The Export Credits Guarantee Department (ECGD), a separate government Department that reports to the Secretary of State for Business, Enterprise & Regulatory Reform, provides a range of products for exporters of such goods and services.

For further information call ECGD on +44 (0)20 7512 7000 or
Visit www.ecgd.gov.uk

Chapter 11: Bribery and Corruption

Business professionals in South Africa may encounter situations which could be viewed as corruption. Sometimes this corruption is overt, such as bribes; in some cases it is more subtle.

Businesspeople may be "wined and dined" or given expensive gifts. This practice is fairly common. However, while not illegal, one could argue about whether or not it is ethical.

It is important for investors to note the difference between clients who want to build a relationship through entertaining investors, and clients who entertain and give gifts to investors expecting something in return.

The unfortunate perception in South Africa in recent years has been that bribery and corruption are the norm. Media attention is forcing those in charge to take a tougher stance.

High-profile corporate leaders have been caught and faced charges in recent years. Our advice to companies encountering corruption is simple: don't get involved. Not only are there issues of business integrity to bear in mind, but it is also, of course, illegal.

The South African Government is keen to crack down on corruption, and penalties can be severe. In addition, under the Anti-Terrorism, Crime and Security Act 2001, UK companies and nationals can now be prosecuted in the UK for acts of bribery or other illegal activity committed wholly overseas.

Bribery is illegal. It is an offence for British nationals or someone who is ordinarily resident in the UK, a body incorporated in the UK or a Scottish partnership, to bribe anywhere in the world.

In addition, a commercial organisation carrying on a business in the UK can be liable for the conduct of a person who is neither a UK national or resident in the UK or a body incorporated or formed in the UK. In this case it does not matter whether the acts or omissions which form part of the offence take place in the UK or elsewhere.

In 2009, South Africa was ranked 55th out of 180 countries in Transparency International's corruption perception index (CPI).

South Africa is a signatory to the OECD Anti-Bribery Convention. The 2010 peer review by members of the Working Group on Bribery found that South Africa had a modern anti-bribery legislation, but more needed to be done on enforcement.

Bribery and corruption is not regarded as endemic in South Africa, but there have been reports and some high level convictions of corruption, in both private and public organisations in South Africa. Any approaches to experiences relating to bribery and corruption in business dealings should be reported to relevant authorities. It should be noted that UK bribery legislation also applies to UK registered companies and UK nationals committing acts of bribery wholly outside the UK.

Chapter 12: Scams and how to Avoid Them

The reason that so many businesses get caught out is that these tricksters are professional, they provide official looking documentation; falsify bank transfers so that victims think money has been transferred into their accounts; they are well groomed, well spoken and seem like professional business people.

The best course of action is to ignore their initial communication. It is also advised that vital documents or information remain secure. As with any business, checking the credentials of potential business partners is of paramount importance.

For further information on various types of scams visit the Office of Fair Trading website, www.oft.gov.uk The promise of easy money has led to a number of unwary business people being caught up in various scams such as the ones listed below:

- Cheque payment fraud or credit card fraud.
- Request for advance fee for registration or pre-qualification for a contract – also known as "419 fraud".
- Transfer of funds from fictitious over-invoiced or failed contracts.
- Promise of phantom contract or supplies.
- Lottery scam that you have won a large sum of money.
- Invitation to share huge amount inherited.
- Request for bank details or bank accounts.

419 scams have a similar pattern. It is often the case that hundreds of emails, letters or faxes are sent out in the hope of snaring one potential victim.

The problems start when the potential victim replies and provides phone numbers, bank account details and other information. The victim will then receive a call in which a profitable deal is put forward. The deal is both "urgent" and "secret" and will require a payment in advance to pay lawyers, bribe corrupt officials or obtain documents.

Official looking documents are then sent to the victim to support the trickster's story and payment request. Pressure is applied saying that there is a chance the deal will fall through unless more money is handed over immediately.

In some cases, victims are invited to go overseas to meet "high-profile" professionals, and further funds may be requested.

Be careful!

Chapter 13: Making Conversation and Meetings

South Africa is a multicultural country with 11 official languages. It is also a popular destination for immigrants from Europe and Asia.

Hence you are likely to interact with people whose home language is not English. Fortunately, English is recognised as the principal language for business communications, and most of the people you deal with will have sufficient command of English.

Entertainment

South Africans are generally outgoing and enjoy entertaining guests. Receptions, events or golf days are often held where business people get to network in a more relaxed atmosphere than in a formal meeting. The host will usually pay for entertainment, but it is always a good idea to offer to pay. A gesture such as offering to split a dinner bill goes a long way in building a better relationship with a client or provider.

Be aware of cultural diversity when entertaining guests; some may have religious or cultural beliefs that prevent them from drinking alcohol or eating certain animal products.

Events and entertainment are important as they help build relationships. Once investors have set up in

South Africa and have a network of business contacts, it is a good idea to reciprocate.

Gifts

It is neither customary nor necessary to give gifts or any tokens of appreciation to potential clients or providers' one meets with. South Africans tend to reserve gifts for those with whom they already have a business relationship.

Meetings

Meetings can range from an informal get-together at a coffee shop to a formal meeting in a company boardroom. It is advisable to get as much information about the planned meeting before the time. Preparation is the key and phone calls should be made to confirm dates and times to avoid misunderstandings.

If a South African tells you they will do something "just now", they mean they'll do it in the near future, not immediately.

And if they say "Now now" they mean shortly, as in: "I will be there now now."

Dress code for meetings in Johannesburg is more formal compared to Cape Town or Durban.

Shaking hands is common for both men and women.

Business cards are usually exchanged by all parties present at meetings. Often, you will meet various representatives from an organisation. It is useful to have more than one contact from each organisation.

Presentations

As a general rule, presentations should be concise, informative and well planned out. It is better to have a shorter presentation, that will allow for a question and answer session afterwards, than a longer presentation that leaves the audience with little time to discuss key points. You should also check media issues in advance such as, for example, if a projector and other audiovisual equipment are available.

Chapter 14: Broad-Based Black Economic Empowerment

Broad-Based Black Economic Empowerment (B-BBEE) is the South African Government's set of policies intended to bring about the involvement or participation of previously disadvantaged communities (PDCs) into the mainstream economy.

The definition of PDCs is people of colour, women of all races, and the disabled. B-BBEE is all about good corporate governance. It does not apply to those who are just exporting goods to South Africa or manufacturing goods for export from South Africa. However, if you intend to set up any kind of business or acquire a running business in South Africa whose annual revenue is likely to exceed R5 million and which will carry out business with government departments, public entities or enterprises, or with companies who supply goods and services to them, you will be asked to provide your B-BBEE status. B-BBEE should be seen as a positive lever to achieve business success in South Africa and not as a deterrent.

The Government is seeking to achieve B-BBEE by:
- increasing the number of PDCs who manage, own and control businesses,
- facilitating the ownership and management of such businesses by communities, workers and other collective enterprises,

- boosting human resource and skills development,
- achieving equitable representation in all categories and levels of the workforce,
- promoting preferential procurement which would involve the purchase of goods and services with a strong B-BBEE score, and
- encouraging investment in enterprises that are PDC-owned or managed.

Any new company setting up in South Africa needs to be aware of this government legislation and regulation that governs B-BBEE. These Acts include the Skills Development Act, the Employment Equity Act, the Preferential Procurement Act and the Broad Based Black Economic Empowerment Act. Companies looking to set up in South Africa should seek professional guidance from a local legal firm and familiarise themselves with the following:

B-BBEE Strategy

Document

This document outlines the South African Government's ten-year B-BBEE plan. It describes the various policies, reasoning behind B-BBEE and means of implementing B-BBEE policies. The document has been produced by the Department of Trade & Industry and is available on its website www.dti.gov.za

Codes of Good Practice

These are the codes that companies can use in order to evaluate and track their B-BBEE efforts. Specific targets need to be met. The codes help businesses get an accurate rating which they can include in their company profile.

Industry Charters

In order to make B-BBEE implementation more effective in each industry, the generic scorecard has been adjusted with weightings that are sector-specific.

Verification

Verification agencies currently use different methods and systems to evaluate a company's empowerment credentials.

The South African National Accreditation System (SANAS) has been appointed by the DTI to devise the criteria for the accreditation of B-BBEE verification agencies, which will in turn standardise systems and ensure consistency and credibility across the verification industry.

Multinationals

There is some confusion about the position of multinational companies, to which the Codes of Good Practice do not currently apply.

In terms of the new codes, equity ownership accounts for 20 points out of 100, but foreign companies will be allowed to accumulate the 100 points through other requirements.

Preferential procurement, skills development and small-business development have been cited as areas in which multinationals can score points. Foreign companies will also have the option of participating in public programmes, which will be regarded as equity equivalents.

Participation will, however, have to equal 25 per cent of their local operations for them to score full ownership points. London-listed companies are specifically excluded, as the codes make it clear that the exemptions do not apply to South African multinationals, for example those headquartered in South Africa.

For further information on B-BBEE visit www.dti.gov.za

Chapter 15: Life Science and Security Opportunities

Life Science Opportunities in South Africa

South Africa consists of a large public health sector and smaller but fast growing private health sector. Despite its size, the public health sector caters for 80% of South Africa's population and has been largely lacking both in infrastructure and human resources. The private health sector on the other hand is well resourced and currently services 20% of the population.

In response to these challenges, the government has increased its spending on public health services from £6.3bn in the 2007/2008 financial year to £11.3bn projected for the 2011/2012 financial year. This 80% increase in just three years is a trend that is expected to continue as the government plans to reduce huge disparities between public and private sector healthcare systems.

These disparities were demonstrated by the difference spent on medicine per person in the previous years, with the public sector spending £6 versus £80 per person in the private sector.

One of the initiatives aimed at closing this gap is the National Health Insurance Scheme. It has required specific funding to be directed towards the revitalization of existing public sector hospitals and improving health systems in order to lay a foundation for its implementation.

Security Opportunities in South Africa

South Africa is a sophisticated and promising market offering a combination of well developed economic infrastructure with a vibrant emerging market economy.

AA Global Sourcing Ltd http://www.aaglobalsourcing.com has identified South Africa as a high growth market and is one of the UK's most significant trading partners, with over £7 Billion in two way trade of goods and services.

South Africa is a member of the Southern African Development Community (SADC), a predominantly trading organisation which represents all African countries south of the Democratic Republic of Congo. As well as trade, security and stability in the region are priorities for SADC.

Through its affiliation to SADC, South Africa is also a member of the Southern African Regional Police Chiefs Co-operation Organisation (SARPCCO), an ACPO style organisation designed to co-ordinate member police services in all aspects of crime, training and criminal procedure.

Counter Terrorism features prominently and minimum standards on CT training were agreed last year. The South African Police Service (SAPS), which numbers about 200,000 police officers and civilian

66

staff, is one of the largest in the world. It has a national remit and is complimented in the larger cities by Metro police and throughout the country by municipal Traffic Departments.

The Service is headed by the National Police Commissioner and each of the nine Provinces has its own Provincial Commissioner. Despite a recent fall in crime, especially violent crime, there are still 47 murders per day across the country and crime involving firearms is widespread.

Border control has recently been taken away from SAPS and given to the South African National Defence force (SANDF).

This was a reflection on SAPS policing priorities lying elsewhere. Nevertheless, illegal immigration by a diverse range of economic and social migrants across the border with Zimbabwe remains a challenge for SAPS.

Crime rates were significantly down during the 2010 FIFA World, unfortunately crime will inevitably rise as the country returns to a semblance of normality.

CCTV technology and coverage in the major cities is generally poor. Enhancing capability is something which both police and civic leaders have longed wished for. UK CCTV technology is admired by many South Africans, both as an investigative tool and crime deterrent.

Examples of major projects Infrastructure

- The ZAR21.9 billion Gautrain project to provide a high speed rail network between Johannesburg and Pretoria.
- Seven new prisons at a cost of ZAR800 million each due to be built to ease current overcrowding. The first facility is under construction in Kimberly, Northern Cape.
- ZAR20 billion spent annually since 2008 on upgrading port and rail services.
- ZAR9 billion spent upgrading roads for 2010 FIFA World Cup. NB Upgrading still continuing despite tournament ending in July 2010.

Maritime Security

The UK and the EU are lobbying for SA to play a greater part in anti-piracy effort in Indian Ocean, especially with Somali pirates now operating off the coast of Mozambique. Any further south and the shipping in an out of the major ports of Durban and Richards Bay will be adversely affected.

South African private security companies are contracted to provide anti piracy security to shipping sailing between South African ports and Suez.

Border Control:

Border control systems upgraded for 2010 FIFA world Cup.
- Border control with Zimbabwe and Mozambique is exploited by sub Saharan

economic and social migrants entering the country illegally.

Doing Business:

There are no significant barriers to doing business in South Africa as most tenders for equipment and services are open to overseas suppliers. What is important is the level of after-sales care available in country. While the security services tend to manage most of their procurements themselves, the SAPS tend to procure their hardware through Armscor (www.armscor.co.za), especially where major capital procurements with an imported content of over US$2 million are concerned, e.g. helicopters from Eurocopter and pistols from Beretta. In these instances an Offset obligation of 50% is placed on the overseas supplier by Armscor and, if the imported content is above US$10 million, then a further obligation of 30% is applied by the DTI.

The DTI enforced obligation, known as the National Industrial Participation Programme (NIPP), applies to all State procurements (goods and services) where the imported content is above US$ 10 million. There is no formal requirement for 3rd party introducers. The South African Government procurers prefer to deal with OEM's on a direct basis though their local Agents are, of course, involved in many instances.

Partnerships are also encouraged, in many instances the preference is for a local "Prime" even where the bulk of the product or technology is coming from abroad. As a result foreign companies bidding for a

SA contract will often sign a teaming agreement with a local company with whom they can cooperate on a commercial or technical basis, i.e. the local company that will maintain and service their equipment post event.

Import duties do apply and the level of duty varies from product to product and whether the product is supplied in completed form, or whether some value add will take place in South Africa.

Chapter 16: Financial Services Opportunities

South Africa's financial services sector has a sound regulatory and legal framework, boasting dozens of domestic and foreign institutions providing a full range of services - commercial, retail and merchant banking, mortgage lending, insurance and investment.

South Africa's banking sector compares favourably with those of industrialised countries. Foreign banks are well represented and electronic banking facilities are extensive, with a nationwide network of automatic teller machines (ATMs) and internet banking facilities available.

The contribution of the financial services sector to GDP has increased over the past decade and stood at 10.4% in 2008. The contribution of mining (10.2%), real estate (6.7%), transport (6.4%), and retail trade (6.2%) are all lower compared to the financial services sector.

The opportunity to use South Africa as a springboard into southern/rest of Africa is not limited to banking. There is increasing demand for African trade and equity deals and UK companies with experience in financial and legal services could look for opportunities to service this market through joint ventures with South African companies.

Another challenge facing the banking sector that provides an opportunity for UK business is the increasing use of international financial markets for debt fund raising and fund management asset growth. PPPs are a key area where the UK has considerable expertise. The infrastructure needs of South Africa exceed the budgets available and so PPPs/PFIs are being increasing seen as the vehicle to deliver the projects. Opportunities exist as both transaction advisers and project financiers.

In the insurance industry, the past year has seen a growth in the registration of niche insurance companies. This is a clear trend and an area of opportunity for specialist providers of insurance products. As with banking, the industry also faces the challenge of insuring low-income earners with innovative new insurance products.

The accounting sector is dominated by the 'big four' international auditing companies, reflecting a worldwide trend. There is a shortage of skills in this sector, but the restrictive practise for Chartered Accountants to operate means that there are opportunities for providing qualifications in accountancy support services.

Islamic banking is another opportunity for UK expertise. Although the South African Islamic finance sector is relatively small, all of the 'big four' banks have Islamic banking departments and there are a couple of Islamic banks, wholly owned by large middle-eastern companies. There is a chronic shortage of skills in this niche sector and there are currently no recognized Sharia banking qualifications.

Chapter 17: Environmental Goods and Services Opportunities

South Africa has yet to fully develop all areas of its environmental industries. Now though the ever increasing pressure on landfill sites, energy and natural resources means it is a market more open than ever to new technologies, management systems and innovation in environmental goods and services.

92% of South Africa's energy comes from coal. 90% of waste in South Africa goes to landfill. The overall size of the South African environmental goods and services market is nearly £2.5billion.

Key areas for development include:
- Waste Management & Recycling
- Air Pollution
- Carbon Capture and Storage
- Environmental Management Systems
- Healthcare Waste
- Water and waste water treatment

The regulations introduced in August 2010 under the National Environment Management Act add to the government's growing awareness in addressing the environmental impact of Africa's largest economy. Meeting the challenging targets laid out is a top priority.

The South African Government has put the environmental sector at the top of its political agenda for the first time.

Waste Management and Recycling

The waste management sector is going to offer huge opportunities for partnerships, technology transfer and consultants, increasingly so as regulatory frameworks are embedded leading to operators having to look to new technology to be able to use/operate alternative disposal methods.

The main challenge for any company wanting to access the South African market offering alternative waste disposal solutions is cost effectiveness. Recycling offers opportunities as industry responds to new legislation which sets a national target to reduce the amount of 'Big 5' waste products (plastics, cans, paper, glass and tyres) going to landfill by 70% by 2022, and to have plans in place to minimise and treat the remaining 30%.

Air Pollution

The main polluters in Johannesburg and Cape Town are household and transport, and in Durban it is those two along with major industries such as mining, refinery and chemicals. A stronger regulatory framework has been needed for a long time and the new NEMA EIA regulations are set to address this.

Carbon Capture and Storage

An atlas of potential underground storage sites for carbon dioxide emissions will be compiled for South Africa as part of a plan to be using carbon capture and storage (CCS) technology by 2020.

The first planned test injection of carbon dioxide is planned for 2016 and a demonstration plant for 2020. The atlas will cost two million South African rand (around US$219,000) while 25 million rand (around US$2.7 million) has been raised for the new centre. The most obvious carbon storage sites are likely to be where gas, oil or coal has been mined.

Environmental Management Systems

There are opportunities in the environmental management systems (EMS) sub sector, as most South African companies are seeking to establish themselves in international markets.

Some are already exporting outside Africa to Europe and the USA. They are pushing to acquire the appropriate ISO accreditation for their businesses to ensure that they meet the international standards required.

Health Care Waste

Health Care Waste processing in SA is orientated towards incineration although there are current discussions for new approaches that would, after treatment, turn medical waste into more general waste. Overseas technologies are extremely welcome as the level of innovation and application in SA is extremely low in this industry.

Water and Waste Water Treatment
See more detail in chapter 18.

Chapter 18: Water Treatment Opportunities

The water services sector in South Africa is large and complex, primarily due to the demographics of the water sector in South Africa and the resultant widespread and large scale transfers of water across catchments that have had to be implemented.

South Africa's inland water resources include 22 major rivers, 264 large dams, more than 4,000 medium and small dams on public and private land, and hundreds of small rivers (source: www.info.gov.uk/aboutsa/water).

The sectors that are the largest users of water in South Africa are agriculture, forestry, industry, mining, power generation and domestic use.

There has been a legacy of inadequate provision of water services to large sections of the South African population due to apartheid.

Progress has been made post-apartheid (1994), but there are still approximately 3 million people that lack access to clean safe water. 15 million people in South Africa (32% of the population) do not have access to basic sanitation, and about 151,660 still use the bucket toilet system. South African Department of Water highlights the critical need for development of new infrastructure.

Skills shortages

There is a huge need for capacity building, providing management and technical support to municipalities. There is a need for skilled engineers, specifically on the design side.
Rand Water highlighted that they currently have to outsource some engineering projects. Rand Water also touched upon the fact that they are looking at Lesotho as a site for future new dams.

TCTA reported that the engineers in South Africa who produce the design information are in the 50+ age bracket, which is not a sustainable position given the future volume of infrastructure work to be implemented in South Africa.

Investment

There is a requirement for private sector involvement in the water and waste water sector in South Africa: asset management; consultancy and training; design, build and operate bulk infrastructure projects.

Department of Water (DoW) reiterated the requirement for private sector infrastructure investment across the water and waste water sector. DoW reported that the South African National Treasury was going to provide an additional R5 billion to address the backlogs.

However, DoW reported that funds to address the backlogs required from private investment were approximately R50 billion. DoW also highlighted the critical need for development of new infrastructure and for rehabilitation and upgrading of the existing infrastructure.

Waste water treatment plants

The South Africa Local Government Association (SALGA) specifically highlighted the waste water sub-sector as an area of serious concern and Rand Water believed it would be beneficial for operators of waste water treatment plants to adopt the franchise model, specifically for the maintenance. In addition, Rand Water (one of the largest water providers in South Africa) is currently looking into a number of potential CDM (clean development mechanism) projects that they could implement at their plants.

Trans-Caledon Tunnel Authority (TCTA)

TCTA are currently involved in a number of major infrastructure projects. TCTA are clear that they would be looking for overseas knowledge, products and services to help them achieve both the creation of the agency, primarily consultancy, and then, going forward, the major task of improving and expanding South Africa's water sector infrastructure.

TCTA highlighted consultancy, innovation and technology as their three key requirements with a focus on:
- Consultancy
- SIM/modelling
- Engineering and design
- Monitoring

- Automation (in purification)
- Education and training
- Project finance support

Water transfer projects

Rand Water felt that within the next 10-20 years larger scale water transfers would need to be considered. Rand Water believe projects similar to the Lesotho Highlands Project would need to be discussed with neighbouring African countries, for example, the Zambezi, which is the largest river close to South Africa.

Rand Water said they were the largest and amongst the better performing water boards in South Africa, currently funding R100 million of renovations and R100 million on new projects through their water tariffs.

Chapter 19: ICT Opportunities

The South African ICT market is the largest in Africa, based on revenue and customers. Nearly 5 million fixed lines are connected. The arrival of broadband services, both fixed and wireless have attracted interest from operators, service providers and end-users and the number of ADSL subscribers now stands at approximately 165,000. With its surging presence in global, political, social and economic systems, ICT plays a significant part in the economic development of the country.

Major role players in South Africa's ICT market include multinationals such as Microsoft, Cisco, Novell, Oracle, SAP, HP, IBM, LG, Dell, Sahara and others, comprising an approximate total value of around £3.8 billion.

The ICT market has been growing consistently over the last seven years. According to the Industrial Development Corporation, the market is predicted to grow at an average annual rate of 11.3% to an estimated £3.8 billion by 2011. IT market growth will be driven by e-government strategies and the implementation of open source software.

South Africa's Telecoms industry is regulated by the Independent Communications Authority of South Africa (ICASA) which is responsible for granting licences, monitoring the competitive environment of the industry and implementing new policies as directed by the Department of Communications

(DoC), the public service arm of the Ministry of Communications.

Despite issues with cost and access, South Africa enjoys the most developed telecoms network in Africa. It is 99.9% digital and includes the latest fixed-line, wireless, satellite and cellular communication. The country also has the 4th largest mobile communications market in the world, with more than 80% of the population having a mobile. The telecoms industry contributes more than 7% to GDP.

Major players:

Vodacom (65% owned by UK company Vodafone), MTN, Cell C and Virgin Mobile (mobile operators) Telkom and Neotel – fixed line operators

Broadcasting:

South Africa has by far the largest television audience in Africa. There are more than nine million households who have licensed televisions. The SABC's national television network comprises four full-spectrum free-to air channels, two satellite pay TV channels aimed at audiences in Africa, and Bop-TV (Zimbabwe), which the SABC runs on behalf of the State. News bulletins are broadcast in all 11 official languages.

Sentech, the broadcasting signal distributor received a £8.8 million allocation from the 2009/10 budget, which will be used to construct a satellite teleport facility in Johannesburg.

The spending follows treasury's £50 million allocation to Telkom in previous year to build a network to connect soccer stadiums to the operator's national network.

Sentech has also been given £14 million to migrate South Africa from analogue to digital terrestrial TV broadcasting. They are, however, facing problems in raising funding for various other projects (including building a wireless broadband network) and will consider engaging with the private sector.

Major players:

The South African Broadcasting Corporation (SABC) and Sentech are responsible for broadcasting infrastructure.

Spending on technology and communications systems was high priority in the 2009/10 budget, including spending on infrastructure for the 2010 FIFA World Cup and for new systems for the South African Police Service and the South African Department of Home Affairs. £260 million has been allocated for a national integrated fingerprint and DNA database to help fight crime and funds have also been allocated to the Department of Home Affairs to upgrade their IT systems to help with modernisation of immigration and customs services at border points.

South Africa is a technically advanced nation with a lot to offer to the international market. The country is, for example, a preferred business destination for Call Centres for UK based companies as South Africa is in the same time zone, the accent is more audible for the British ear and the currency exchange is very attractive to UK companies.

The Education and Training sector has presented a number of opportunities for UK ICT products and service suppliers. Both state and private institutions of education have shown an interest in products like interactive whiteboards and online training and assessment programmes.

Opportunities for CRM applications and services are present and potential clients include local authorities and municipalities in need of efficient, transparent and user-friendly systems to manage their customers and billings and payment systems. Furthermore, various departments within a municipality require CRM energy, transport, traffic and water etc) to have a single view of the customer.

Compliance with regulatory and various other corporate governance requirements place increasing pressure on companies to deploy technologies that will simplify the company's ability to demonstrate compliance. Security and storage solutions are also in demand.

According to the IT research firm, BMI-T, the small and medium size enterprise (SME) market displays significant demand for IT products and services with hardware and software demand leading demand. The development of SMEs is strongly encouraged by the South African Government as a means to achieve the government's key socioeconomic objectives of skills development, job creation and poverty alleviation.

There are ample opportunities in the wireless application services market as network operators have recently seen the market open up in terms of legislation. Although Telkom and Neotel were South Africa's fixed line operators, the recent Altech Autopage court ruling has opened up market competition for other network operators. This ruling now allows VANS licence holders to develop their own telecommunications networks independently of other licensed infrastructure operators, therefore not having to operate as resellers.

The Broadband Infraco Bill of 2007 (www.pmg.org.za/bills/070705b26-07.pdf) focuses on optimising access to broadband in South Africa's rural areas. Infraco is a state owned investment intervention that will allow government to leverage ICT infrastructure for economic growth, ultimately bringing broadband to the nation's under-developed and under-serviced areas.

With internet connectivity and access to broadband, the availability of technology is not the issue, but rather how it is used and implemented. This situation is likely to improve dramatically with the completion of the second fibre optic cable to connect East and southern Africa with India and Europe.

The cable, which spans international waters of 11 different countries, is being constructed by US firm SEACOM, with hopes that it will dramatically increase internet connectivity and access to broadband and lower costs. Currently, 85% of all internet clicks on South Africa are for international websites; an indication of opportunities for international companies in the market.

Many South African internet service providers have bought into the SEACOM cable which will also lead to better quality services.

In 2011, Digital Terrestrial Broadcasting (DTT) was launched in order to keep up with world trends. Therefore, South Africans will need digital decoders to access new channels as the move away from analogue broadcasting is implemented.

Chapter 20: Political and Economic Situation

Political Situation

South Africa is a young, yet stable democracy, dominated by one political party. The African National Congress (ANC) has won all four national elections since the start of democracy in 1994. Jacob Zuma became president in May 2009 following the ANC's victory at the polls securing 65.9% of the popular vote. He came to power with the support of the tripartite alliance consisting of the South African Communist Party (SACP), the Congress of South African Trade Unions (COSATU) and the ANC.

Although the ANC recently won 63% of the vote in the May 2011 Local Government Elections, the main opposition party, the Democratic Alliance, was deemed the biggest winner as it increased its support base from 14% in 2006 to 25%. This gives the opposition a solid platform to intensify their campaign and strengthen their bid for the 2014 national election.

Despite the ANC's domination of South African politics, diverse interests within and between the tripartite alliance creates its own checks and balances. Calls from the left for a more radical approach to economic policy, including greater government intervention to create employment, competes with the views of economic moderates who emphasize the importance of prudent monetary and fiscal economic policy.

Economic Situation

South Africa has recovered from its first recession in 17 years after it contracted by 1.7% in 2009 on the back of the collapse in global trade. Prudent macroeconomic policies and tight banking regulation limited the impact of the global downturn. And years of fiscal responsibility provided the space to respond effectively to the crisis. Economic growth in 2011 has continued its momentum from the end of 2010. Annualized growth of 4.8% in Q1 of 2011 surpassed expectations and increased from 4.5% in Q4 2010. The National Treasury forecasts growth of 3.4% for 2011 increasing to 4.4% by 2013.

The economy is diversified, with a strong services sector. Finance, real estate and business services are the largest industry contributing 20.7% to GDP and manufacturing contributes 16.4%. While manufacturing was the best performing industry during Q1, exporters continue to blame the strong, and some argue, overvalued Rand for eroding their international competitiveness. Mining only contributes 5.5% to GDP, but it is important for employment and is a significant foreign exchange earner.

Unemployment remains an immense challenge with an official figure of 25% but the real figure is probably nearer 40%. Two thirds of all those unemployed are below the age of 35. President Zuma announced during his speech at the 99th anniversary of the ANC that 2011 would be the year of job creation. He officially endorsed the 'New Growth Path' document that aims to create 5 million jobs in 10 years. In addition, a new jobs fund has been announced and a youth wage subsidy is in the pipeline.

Key challenges for the year ahead will come from chronic skills shortages, low productivity levels and infrastructure bottlenecks particularly in energy, transport and water which are a result from years of underinvestment.

South Africa has an inflation target band of 3-6%, but this framework is heavily criticized by the left. Inflation bottomed out at 3.2% in September 2010 and has been climbing slowly since. External cost push factors of high fuel and food prices have taken the blame. Domestic factors of double digit increases in electricity and significantly above inflation wage increases are expected to add further pressure. Inflation is expected to stay within the band during the year with the SARB forecasting 5.1% for 2011 and 6% for 2012. The Reserve Bank has cut the repo rate by 6.5 ppt since December 2008 to 5.5% but could start tightening before the end of the year.

South Africa is an ideal export market for UK companies and is fourth on the list of key emerging markets for global investors. The South African Government has embarked on an ambitious multi-year capital expenditure programme worth approximately £90 billion, with the majority of the spending taking place in public infrastructure and power generation.

South Africa has recently joined the BRICS grouping and China is South Africa's largest trading partner, although the UK is in the top 5. UK exports to South Africa in 2010 were worth £3.5 billion, while imports from South Africa totalled £4.4 billion. Some 600 South African companies are present in the UK (4 out of 5 South African businesses in Europe are based in the UK). Both countries are committed to the bilateral government agreement to double trade by 2015.

Terrorism Threat

There is an underlying threat from terrorism. Attacks, although unlikely, could be indiscriminate, including in places frequented by expatriates and foreign travellers.

South Africa has a high level of crime and visitors should be vigilant about personal security and when driving around the country. Please consult FCO travel advice for up-to-date information about the situation.

Visitors to South Africa should be diligent about protecting digital data. Spyware, phishing and malicious software tools are common. One example of this is to send authentic-looking emails to potential victims. The emails appear to have been sent from a trusted institution such as a bank, requesting recipients to divulge personal information. Once criminals have these details they are able to steal money from the victims' bank accounts. Diligence coupled with firewalls or spyware removal tools are recommended.

Chapter 21: Conclusion

South Africa's National Planning Commission "Vision for 2030" is an ambitious plan for tackling the country's major problems. Its success hangs on strong leadership and willingness to challenge entrenched interests. Some potential for UK companies to capitalise on infrastructure programmes and for stronger joint working on climate change, health and regional integration.

In mid November 2011, the National Planning Commission (NPC) released its National Development Plan: Vision for 2030 (NDP). The document attempts to identify solutions to the challenges facing South Africa set out in the Commission's earlier diagnostic report including high unemployment, low levels of education and high inequality.

Long term vision needed to channel troubled waters

It is 17 years since South Africa's first democratic election. This seems a long time for many living in poverty for whom the outlook remains bleak. The official unemployment rate is high at 25% and unofficial estimates put it as high as 40%. Two thirds of all unemployed are below the age of 35; youth unemployment is, as Deputy President Kgalema Motlanthe puts it, a ticking time bomb. The NPC's earlier diagnostic report illustrates the stark reality: people face a lifetime of unemployment if they have not worked by the age of 30.

The diagnostic report highlighted the need for a long term vision that captures the country's imagination and unites people behind the common goal of lowering unemployment and decreasing inequality.

Vision for 2030

The 444 page plan, which included extensive research by the 26 National Planning Commissioners, sets clear but ambitious targets for 2030. These include lifting the current 39% of households living in poverty to above the poverty threshold and bringing the Gini coefficient measure of inequality down from 0.7% to 0.6%. The plan consists of 15 topic specific chapters, including economy and employment, infrastructure, health, education, South Africa's position in the world and a low carbon economy. Each chapter lists specific targets and action points to guide implementation.

Tackling unemployment is at the heart of the NDP. The economy needs an additional 11 million jobs to bring unemployment down to 6% by 2030. The NDP estimates that the country needs to grow at an average annual rate of 5.4% to make inroads into employment creation. But an increase in the current growth rate alone is not sufficient. The NDP emphasises that expanding employment should take precedence over improving living standards of those already employed.

The plan notes that sustainable job creating growth will require major structural changes. It proposes an increase in exports of products and services in areas where the country has a competitive advantage, such as mining, construction, agriculture, agro-processing and tourism. It singles out the opportunities to increase production of niche products e.g. cherries, to capture a larger share of global demand.

Just another plan?

The NDP is the latest of several major development plans since 1994. The NDP's success depends on strong leadership from government, labour, business and civil society. Some believe that the document tries to cover too many objectives instead of opting to tackle a couple of important, contentious issues. Other commentators question the NDP's focus on exports. They doubt the country's ability to be internationally competitive in manufactured products and fear that this attempt at a fundamental structural change could fail.

Zuma set up the NPC when he came into power in 2009 as a commission and not a department; its Chairman, former Finance Minister, Trevor Manuel has stressed its "advisory function". So the implementation of the NDP will fall to others.

Implications for the UK

A stronger more prosperous South Africa would strengthen the region and decrease regional dependence on aid. Improved regional economic conditions coupled with better infrastructure and elimination of non tariff barriers within the region (as identified in the NDP) would increase the market access for UK products. The NDP indicates the long term need for extensive infrastructure development in key sectors such as transport, energy and water. This could potentially provide long term opportunities for UK companies.

It is also welcome to see the strong focus on a low carbon transition running through all sections of the NDP. The section on climate change specifically refers to the breadth and depth of stakeholder consultation.

Our Comment

South African public and media reactions to the NDP have been mixed and pretty muted. Most commentators have welcomed the plan's seriousness and broad direction: there is broad consensus on what South Africa's underlying economic and social problems are. But the Commission itself has no power to force through its recommendations and it will be for President Zuma and his Cabinet Ministers to do the heavy lifting necessary to turn ideas into action.

Good Luck!